5 THINGS I LOVE ABOUT YOU

PRAISE FOR PETRA'S BOOKS

"I love this book! I would recommend this book to anyone and everyone. It is a total life-changer! We must choose joy every day and this book gives us the tools we need to be successful. This experience has definitely motivated my mind and inspired my heart. I truly needed this book to capture myself."

- Sylva, Chili & Chocolate Blogger, Czech

"I have never come across a book written with so much enthusiasm, strong knowing of the power of CHOICE and how to create that in your life! Louise Hay started the affirmation movement but this book is designed in a way so that when you read it you are already saying the affirmations much less learning how to act as if they were and are already true. It is the kind of book I have on coffee table by bed so I can read a chapter in 5-10 minutes if feeling blue or unsure about life, reminding myself who I really am and all I can BE on this planet! Love it!"

-Margaret, Naturopathic Doctor, USA

"I love myself so much more after reading this book. As soon as I finished it, I started reading it again. It has given me so much personal power and self worth. I am so grateful I bought this book and met Petra in person."

- Yorgi, Yoga Geek, Germany

"I have just finished your book and wanted to tell you how grateful I was to have crossed your way. Your words were awakening ideas that I already know somehow but so good to hear it this way. They have been nourishing my thoughts and heart lately. Thank you."

- Aline, Australia

"I found your book '5 Things I Love About You' and it was the best gift I could find before hosting my first yoga retreat. You described in beautiful words what I wanted to share with my yoga tribe. A few days into my retreat, I found another book of yours, 'I Am Amazing' and had to buy it immediately. Some of my students followed me and bought the book too. I just finished reading it and I am beyond grateful that I found it. You really inspire me and you write about so many things I totally believe in! Thank you for sharing your awesomeness with this world. I love learning more from you!"

- **Audrey, Yoga Teacher, Austria**

"Thank you for shining your AWESOMENESS, your AMAZINGNESS and your ROCKSTAR attitude into the words of this book! It was life-changing for me at a time when I truly felt the world was not on my side. I keep this book with me all the time as it is my bible, my life saver, my life changer and my life up-leveler. Thank you and stay cool my sista!!"

- **Lizzy, Champion Ski Racer, Canada**

"Thank you for the positive impact you have had on my life. I'm relishing a lot of fabulous thoughts and notions from all kinds of sources now, and it all started with your book, so I'm really grateful. This morning, I got up to see the sun rise over the sea and then went for a run, soaking up all the beautiful nature along the way. Life is good and I can really appreciate it due to your book!"

- **Johanna, Spain**

"A feel-good read, bursting with energy and positivity. This book has played an important part in my journey of self-discovery and happiness for which I am really grateful."

- **Scott, Head Chief Animation School, Canada**

"I've finished your book! Loved it and was sad to finish it as I so enjoyed reading it. Am recommending it to some friends I know will cherish it too. I've started a journal and have always practiced gratitude but now am listing 10 things when I wake up. So much in your book I had a huge connection with. Thank you from my heart. Your book came to me at exactly the right time and as you so rightly said, there are no coincidences."

- **Rachel, Pilates Personal Trainer, Spain**

"I can tell this book is written by a woman who understands the importance of self-care through intense personal experience. She has helped me and my friends change the way we see ourselves. She is amazing and I now carry Petra's mantra, 'Unfold your wings and fly'. I can't wait for the newest book to arrive."

- **Denise, Hotel Owner, Indonesia**

"Very uplifting book that definitely raised my vibration! This book and the author are so positive. Anyone who is struggling with self-love and self-compassion would find this book useful. I highly recommend giving it a try."

- **Rebecca, Pro Surfer, Hawaii**

"Petra, you truly radiate light and love and all that is good in the world. You ARE amazing, thanks for being that beacon of hope and swagger, reminding us that we are truly special. Love your juicy cleansing and this just makes me want even MORE from you. Thank you, You ROCK!"

- **Pat, Life & Business Coach, New York**

"A positive and powerful way to live! This book is my bible and one to keep close. So happy I read it."

- **Ginger, Movie Script Supervisor, Canada**

"This book is amazing!!!! When I look in the mirror and say the title out loud, I feel the truth resonating from the top of my head to the bottom of my feet. My personal doubts slowly disappeared upon reading this book and I really am able to do anything I ever wanted to do. Thank you Petra for sharing your amazing truth and helping wake the world up and heal all of our wounded hearts. I am ready to love myself more and I am so happy I read this book."

- **Rick, Hypnotherapist & Spiritual Alchemist, Arizona**

"This book was bought as a gift and I loved it! So many things Petra writes resonates with me on a deep level. Upon reading it, I learned so much, I had so many ideas, I felt so many emotions and it really opened me up. This was a life changing book for me and will always be so special."

- **Nedi, Morning News Producer, Africa**

"Fantastic book, especially whenever I need a positive charge! Petra's words literally seethe right off the page and I cannot help but smile. I believe in myself more and more as I read the words like mantras. Easy to read, down-to-earth and authentic! I highly recommended it!"

- **Pamela, Coffee Barista, Amsterdam**

"Petra is an amazing being. She is always uplifting, great sense of humor, speaks straight to the point and is fantastic chef! She is courageous and dedicated to her mission to heal the world and empower the women. Petra walks her talk. This book is beautiful, funny and authentic."

- **Mariola, Yogini & Model, Hawaii**

5 THINGS I

LOVE

ABOUT YOU

A Game For You To Heal Your Relationships
With Everyone

PETRA EATJUICY
Green Smoothie Gangster

5 THINGS I LOVE ABOUT YOU

At your core you want to be seen, loved, heard, received, gotten and supported. This book will help you get there.

ISBN 9781983276675

Book cover by: Petra EatJuicy & Adityah Kasim
Book layout by: Petra EatJuicy & Adityah Kasim

Visit me on the web!
www.EatJuicy.com
www.GreenSmoothieGangster.com

Tell me how you liked the book!
www.Facebook.com/PetraEatJuicy

First Edition: 2017

THANK YOU FOR BUYING THIS BOOK.

TIME TO FULFILL YOUR DEEPEST DESIRE OF CONNECTION,
INTIMACY, FRIENDSHIP, LOVERSHIP & FAMILY.

THIS BOOK IS ONE TOOL TO GET YOU THERE, ALL YOU HAVE TO
DO IS BE BRAVE ENOUGH TO PLAY. IT'S A GAME YOU PLAY WITH
OTHERS AND IT WORKS....TRY IT.

FREE VIDEO LESSONS & RECIPES AT

www.EatJuicy.com
www.GreenSmoothieGangster.com

www.Facebook.com/PetraEatJuicy
www.Youtube.com/PetraEatJuicy
www.Instagram.com/PetraEatJuicy

THIS BOOK IS DEDICATED TO YOU MY FAMILY.
I CREATED THIS GAME FOR YOU, SO WE CAN ALWAYS
REMEMBER HOW MUCH WE LOVE EACH OTHER.

AND

THIS BOOK IS ALSO DEDICATED TO YOU AND YOUR FAMILIES.
IT'S TIME TO HAVE THE MOST PEACEFUL, HAPPY, HEALED
AND SAFE RELATIONSHIPS WITH EVERYONE IN YOUR LIFE.
THIS GAME WILL HELP YOU GET THERE...
HAVE FUN PLAYING!

CONTENTS

CHAPTER 1

How This Game /
Act of Love Was
Created

14 YEARS AGO my mom died of cancer and my family got spun for quite a loop. We, the HALUSKA family of 4, were quite close. We went to Czech dances together, went to events together, had each other over for dinners, celebrated Christmases together, travelled together, camped together, partied together and watched movies cuddled on the couch together.

In 1979 we escaped from Communist, Czech Republic along with another foursome family. We left everything and told no one, so the communists wouldn't find out. During a special moment in time, the European borders opened up and allowed people to travel out of their country. This is the moment my parents planned, a few months in advance and one weekend we set out for a beach vacation and never came back. We crossed into the Austrian border, which supported immigrants and were immediately taken care of, housed, fed and clothed. We lived in Austria for 10 months in the most beautiful, family run country side Austrian Hotel with other Czech escapees also waiting for permission to immigrate to a new country.

10 months later and me now speaking fluent German (as I was only 8 and quick to pick up languages), we got permission to come to Canada. My parents, then 34, knew no English and knew no one in Canada. Super brave souls looking for a better life for themselves and for their kids, they let go of everything they knew and owned, and flew to the foreign land of freedom, Canada.

The funniest story I loved hearing from my parents was, upon arriving into Canada and being given a home at English Bay Beach Hotel in fabulous Vancouver, British Columbia, they put us kids to bed and decided to sneak out for a celebratory beer. In the Czech Republic it is common to buy beers at little convenience stores. So my mom and dad stepped into one and unknowingly bought something called root beer, excited to cheers their new life and new found freedom. The funniest is their recount of their first big swig of what they thought was Canadian beer and quickly spat out this disgusting liquid. It was much later in their Canada stay they realized, they had bought soda pop instead of beer.

So my Haluska family and I made Canada our new home. We were happy, travelled, had many new friends and loved our life. Then 14 years ago, my mom was diagnosed with cancer and died 3 months later. Our family and hearts fell to pieces.

After my mom died, there just wasn't as much love and peace between all of us. We still loved each other, but the energy was missing. I quickly saw how my mom was the beacon we all revolved around and how she held us all together. I took on this role, but would find myself incredibly sad and discouraged by the lack of yum that was amongst us.

I moved to Hawaii and lived there for 5 years. As a Canadian, I was able to stay for 6 months and always flew back to Canada for the breaks. I dreaded it every time. In 2013, I moved to Bali Indonesia having fallen in love with yet another island. In 2014, I created the Green Smoothie Gangster Tour and toured the West Coast of the United States for 7 months. I teamed up with grocery stores and handed out green smoothie samples in their stores. I would get people turned on to the power of green smoothies and sign them up for my online Healthy, Juicy, Amazing Lifestyle Club to empower and help them take their health into their hands, feel amazing inside and love themselves a whole lot more. Lots of people signed up... and my tribe grew.

As my Tour was finishing, I was again dreading my Canada return and the Haluska Family Christmas. So one day on my Tour, as I camped last minute in the Red Wood Forest to hide from the dark rainy windy storm and after listening to Marianne Williamson read her book, "A Return To Love" on Youtube,

I prayed to the Gods, Angels, Fairies, Ethereal Beings and to my MOMMA and asked for a miracle to bring my family back together.

What I heard was, "create a game called 5 Things I LOVE About YOU and play it with each person in the family. Then also play it as a group during Christmas." I said YES.

So upon returning to Canada, I kept my promise and with a nervous beating heart started to play this game with each of my family members. The results were astonishing. The energy shift was extremely powerful. My nephew, Anthony, and I would play during our sleep overs and he absolutely loved it. I knew I had a hit and knew it was the healing my family needed.

All too often, we live with people or have people in our lives and we don't express our love for them. We rarely tell the intimate people in our lives what we love about them and we rarely hear it back from them. We assume we know, but we don't.

We all need a little healing in the relationships we have with others, so I am sharing with you this simple yet super powerful game so you may heal your relationships and reconnect deeper with your loved ones. Deeper, more meaningful connection with people in your life is what you truly want most.

It is your birthright to be happy, at peace, abundant, loved and safe. Go create it.

You are POWERFUL!!! YOU CAN DO IT! I am behind you. I got your back and I'm happy to guide you to a happier land.

Let's do this. With much love and aloha,
Petra

It is your birthright
to be happy
at peace
abundant
loved and safe
Go create it

. . .

CHAPTER 2

How The Game Started To Take Form

PLAYED THE GAME FIRST with my sister in law, Angie. We both loved each other, yet never told each other why and so on one level we questioned the deepness of our connection. I was nervous as heck. I didn't know what she would think about playing. I didn't know if she would say yes. With my heart beating like crazy, I put myself out there. OF COURSE it went awesome and love gushed between us. Both of us were surprised and deeply touched by what we each shared and gave each other a huge hug to follow.

This was a great start, I thought. I had more confidence in myself, in this game and in my words. I was ready for the next person.

Now I must say here, that most of the time I came home to Canada knowing I needed to be big LOVE. I hold a lot of love energy and gave it freely, as I felt everyone around me really needed it and were quite starving for it. With my highly developed self love and my deep understanding of human consciousness, I would arrive to Canada feeding light and love to all those around me. I was no longer seeking love outside of myself and knew my family was struggling to find their own self love.

Yet even though I didn't need it, the lack of love and affirmative language from others would eventually drain me. So this game allowed me to give love and receive it at the same time. I was able to fuel others and in return I too was fueled. It felt like such a win win and beautiful way of connecting to those I love.

My next player was my nephew, Anthony. We played while having sleep overs in my big guest bed. He would ask me to scratch his back and draw circles on it. Then massage his hands because as he says, I am the best masseuse ever. We would play 5 Things I LOVE About YOU with each other and about all the people we knew. It was so fun to do it with a little being so filled with unconditional love for himself and for others.

With Anthony on board I knew I had a hit....

I played with others, my brother, my dad, my step momma and friends. This game filled everyone with love and filled me with love too. I realized how much everyone craved verbal affirmation and a positive mirror to witness themselves. I also saw how much everyone loved to give this positive energy to me, even when they were shy and afraid of their own loving words. I realized this game was going to take practice and bring people skills of verbal love connection. I realized that this game would be able to heal even the deepest chasms in relationships and bring people closer to what they truly desire at their core...deep intimate safe loving human connection.

The importance of this game, 5 Things I LOVE About YOU, was growing and I knew it would help people have more light and love in their life. It is always my purpose to LIGHTEN / ENLIGHTEN humanity and this book has become another tool to do so. May you have the courage to bring this game into your homes to heal your relationships and to help us save the world with LOVE.

I know by shining my light and showing you the way, I will give you permission to shine your light too and help make your life that much more extraordinary.

YOU ARE POWERFUL

YOU ARE AMAZING

YOU ARE LOVED

SPREAD YOUR LOVE

TO THOSE YOU LOVE

SO THEY CAN SPREAD THEIR LOVE

TO THOSE THEY LOVE

AND OUR WORLD WILL BE

FILLED WITH MORE LOVE

. . .

CHAPTER 3

The Czech Christmas Traditions

VERY QUICKLY INTO MY VANCOUVER TRIP, I knew I was brave enough to play the 5 Things I LOVE About You game at Christmas and enroll everyone in. My family loved each other, yet were distant. We were in a displaced place. We craved more love from each other than we gave and kept each other at an arm's length on many levels. I knew that a game of love and truth would save my family from separation. I knew I held the key to pull my family together. The power of praise and appreciation transforms relationships. I would soon see how this game would transform my family and the energy between us.

Before I tell you how to play the game, I will share with you a little about our Czech Christmas and how it is celebrated as I find the various cultural traditions fascinating and would love to share mine with you.

We get together on Christmas Eve, the 24th, as is our Czech tradition. We also put our presents under the tree right before we open them. The little kids and some of us big kids, go into the bedroom and wait for JESUS to deliver the presents. He rings a bell and we know he has come. We don't have Santa Claus coming down the chimney, as is the western world. We have Jesus coming through the window delivering presents. I see him as a baby cherub, yet others have different interpretations. The man in a red suit does not exist for us.

We do have a Czech Santa though, who shows up at Christmas parties along with a furry black devil and a white angel. He is dressed in white, with a tall white hat, with a cross on the front and looks more like the pope. The Czech devil is a black furry creature who has hoofs, big horns and rattles a big chain. He is covered in ash from the coal of fires. The white angel represents the good and the devil represents the bad. The angel hands out candy and the devil hands out coal.

Czech's celebrate with a dinner on the 24th followed by a present opening extravaganza. There are no stockings. There are presents under a REAL tree, usually put up Christmas eve at the same time as the presents, while us children are waiting in the bedroom. That's right! My mom and dad would put up the entire tree, the night of Christmas eve and pull out all the presents to create the wow factor for us kids.

It is always a really magical experience to enter into the living room and experience the biggest sensation of WOW! To see a lit up tree with presents all underneath it, where hours before there was nothing, is quite a wondrous experience for a kid of any size. So for a long time we kept our tradition of waiting in the bedroom for a tree and presents to appear. Eventually we went with western culture and put up our tree in early December. I can understand that for my mom it was a lot to pull together in a few hours and it became fun to create the tree together. Yet, we still believe in the WOW factor and put our presents under the tree the night of Christmas eve. I invite you to add more WOW into your Christmas traditions and wait till last minute to put the presents under the tree too. Especially for little kids, it is a wondrous experience.

Czechs eat breaded carp fish for dinner along with homemade perfectly cubed potato salad with peas, carrots and little cubed pickles. Our first Christmas in Canada, we had a carp fish swimming in our bathtub for a few days prior. Yes, a live fish swimming in our bathtub. Such is the Czech tradition to buy a live carp fish and kill it for Christmas dinner. So my dad killed the fish. He gave me the scales, as they appeared like translucent glittery mermaid coins. He is also grabbed the dead fish several times and pretended it was a puppet talking to me and tried chasing me with it. Of course I squealed and loved every minute of playing with my dad. Always.

This was our Christmas meal for years 35 + years of our Canada residency. My dad added breaded giant prawns into this dinner and made those for years and years. Until last year, when

I was in Australia during Christmas, I heard the Christmas dinner transitioned to no flour, no gluten, no fried food, new raw desserts and the addition of a green kick ass salad. Oh how excited I am to experience this new tradition as I travel home for Christmas this year.

We will again play the 5 Things I LOVE About YOU game.

CHAPTER 4

The Game And Christmas

I HAD BEEN DISCUSSING WITH MY NEPHEW, Anthony, leading up to Christmas that we were going to unveil this game for the whole family and we would do it together. He was in.

I mentioned to my sister in law, Angie, that we would all play the game after Christmas dinner. She was in agreement. I felt more confident having a support team and was ready for our family transformation.

So after dinner and after presents, I pulled out a big bowl and told everyone we were playing a game together. I told them I had our names on pieces of paper in this bowl and I would pull a name out. This was the person in receiving that would get love from everyone and then I would draw another name. I told them about the game and the simplicity of how we would play.

My dad instantly stood up and said, "No. I am not playing." He got up and went into the kitchen to sit at the computer to distract himself. I understood his hesitation and fear, and released any expectations. Then my brother stood up and wanted his son, Anthony, to go do jiujutsu with him downstairs. I objected and stated that this was mine and Anthony's game and if he wanted to go downstairs alone, that was fine but Anthony was staying to play. With restless energy and unease, my brother sat back down on the couch. I again understood his uncomfortableness and released any expectations of him being ready or emotionally available to play this simple, yet powerful game.

We started to play. I pulled a name. We took turns. We spoke kindness to each other and our hearts opened. The givers felt good for giving. The receivers felt good receiving and did their best to receive without attempting to deflect. The kids loved it. It was perfect exactly as it was, divinely orchestrated for everyone's highest healing.

Then the most miraculous thing happened. My dad got bored of the computer and started walking back into the living room. I reached into the bowl for the last name to be drawn and of course it was his. So I said, "oh wow look dad, it is your turn. Sit down and receive our love." We all took turns and shared love for my dad. He loved it, glowed and felt really yummy in his heart. He was uncomfortable to give but felt good to receive. It was perfect.

Perfect timing orchestrated perfectly by the angels, my momma and the amazing universe. The miracle of healing I asked for, was granted to me. My family spoke love to each other. Love that we had not spoken before and we found the courage that night to speak it. Everyone's heart's opened even more.

I AM GRATEFUL THAT THE UNIVERSE HAS MY BACK.
IT HAS YOURS TOO.

SO ARE YOU READY TO PLAY?

. . .

CHAPTER 5

How Do You Play?

I'T'S REALLY QUITE SIMPLE, yet everything that goes with this game is complex. The amount of energy this simple game can shift is tremendous and you hold a lot of power if you are ready to play it with those you love. You have the power to transform any relationship with conversation. Your words hold a lot of power and the intention behind those words is even more powerful.

Most conversations between people are spoken head to head, brain to brain, talking and more talking. Our egos are involved and we are usually thinking, analyzing and assuming more than we are listening.

So let's move down to our heart. Science has proven that our heart is our other brain and is even more powerful. It too can govern our body and when we are governed from our heart, we live our life, much more in love. This game comes from your heart. In order to play with the most authenticity and integrity, you have to drop down to your heart and speak from this brain instead of the one in your head. When you speak to someone from your heart, it is received in to their heart and you both feel yummy.

So let's drop down to our heart...

How you play is super simple. You sit down with your loved one and you say, "hey do you want to play this game with me? Let's tell each other 5 things we love about each other."

The other person agrees and one of you starts. Usually it's you since you can lead better by example.

What you say is, "(Person's Name), the first thing I love about you is......"

Then you say, "(Person's Name), the second thing I love about you is......"

Then you say, "(Person's Name), the third thing I love about you is......"

Then you say, "(Person's Name), the fourth thing I love about you is......"

Then you say, "(Person's Name), the fifth thing I love about you is......"

And then you trade. Simple right? Yet it is emotionally complex. Read on as I guide you through playing this game on a deeper level.

CHAPTER 6

Receiving

THE HARDEST PART OF THIS GAME for most people is receiving. By receiving I mean hearing positive, encouraging, loving, empowering, inspiring, high vibrational reflections of their greatness. This is the hardest part for most people to deal with. Why?

Because most people don't believe it about themselves and they feel unworthy to align themselves with this reflection. They will likely deflect it, verbally out loud or internal inside their head. Somewhere they don't believe what you are saying is true. They will think, "no you don't really believe that about me. You are lying or you are embellishing. I don't believe these words you are saying about me to really be true".

Playing this game can bring up a lot of emotional crap for people if they are not resolved with their issues or comfortable with themselves. Some people will not want to play because they will not want to hear this high vibrational truth. Truth that reminds them of how glorious, miraculous and beautiful they are. They will want to cling to their smallness, their inabilities and their ugliness a little longer.

So the first most important part of playing this game is being able to open up and receive all the goodness that is coming your way. Open up your heart, stretch your arms open wide and expand your chest to receive all the love. You may have to listen to that disbelieving belittling voice inside your head that will tell you the positive words are not true and you have got to shut that voice up.

It is the smallness that is not true. You are clinging to an old program or belief system of fear, scarcity and self hate. Time to drop it. It is no longer serving you and it is not true. No matter how you have shown up in this world to this date, you are a good person. You have a big heart and you deserve to be happy. It is your birthright to be happy and to be loved. So open up your heart and let the love in. It is all around you, time you start seeing it.

There are so many yummy reasons I love this game and opening you up to receiving is my favorite part. I believe all of us are on a journey in this lifetime to learn 2 things, self love and receiving. Everything you want is all around you, you just have to have the courage to open yourself up enough to receive it and you have to love yourself enough to feel worthy to let all that goodness in.

So open up and let it all in. RECEIVE all the good! It is your birthright to have a wonderful, happy and blissful life. LOVE YOURSELF enough to give it to yourself. NOW!!

CHAPTER 7

Giving

FOR SOME PEOPLE GIVING IS VERY EASY, sometimes so easy that they feel only comfortable to give and never allow themselves to receive. They give and give out of love for others, yet lack the love for themselves to receive the love back. It is a wonderful feeling to give, yet please find your balance and allow yourself to have both.

For some people giving love and speaking empowering statements to others, is very difficult. For them, being able to express them selves and drop into their emotions is too challenging and they would rather not bring themselves there. They live more comfortably in the head and feel fearful dropping down into their heart.

This is why this game is so powerful, as it is teaching both aspects of give and receive. It also teaches you to drop down into your heart, where you are perhaps too afraid to go. Life is more fun when you have access to your heart and when you can drop into this place.

So how do you do this? How do you drop into your heart? You start feeling the love you have for this person. You start feeling the gratitude you feel for having them in your life. You start thinking of everything you love and appreciate about them and their personality. You connect to the loving beautiful thoughts you have about yourself or anyone else in your life. You start focusing your energy and tuning into your LOVE frequency.

Then from this love place, you say 5 Things You LOVE About Them and you give them love. You make this about THEM. What do you love about THEM? Love about THEIR personality? Love about their physical appearance? Love about their internal soul and internal heart? Love about how they show up in this world?

Don't make this about yourself. Even if you are grateful for how they helped you, supported you, loved you, saved you or inspired you, change the language to reflect them. Remind them of their greatness. Reflect back to them their personality. Tell them how you see them in the world. Be the most empowering and inspiring mirror for them possible.

It is ok to include physical things you love about someone. Their hair, eyes, lips and body, yet don't make it all about their physical appearance. People are more moved when you see them on the inside. Everyone can say they have beautiful hair but can you tell them they have a beautiful soul? This is what most people crave, to be seen on a deeper level and appreciated for the fire they have inside.

This is where magic happens, when you can witness another in a way they may have not been witnessed before. They might think no one noticed this greatness and when you verbally tell them, their heart swells up with yum. Allow yourself to be a source of magical inspiration for another and to witness their depth. They will super appreciate hearing it, even if it shocks them in to receiving it.

When you give from your heart, it will touch their heart. You can give one word, one sentence or small paragraph. How much you give is up to you. Make your message clear. Remember the most important part of this giving, is the other person. So give for them. Set the intention that the 5 Things You LOVE About Them will empower, inspire and lift them up.

YES, YOU ARE THIS POWERFUL.
YES, YOU HAVE THIS POWER TO MAKE
A MASSIVE POSITIVE FOOTPRINT ON
SOMEONE'S LIFE FOR A DAY
OR FOR THEIR LIFETIME.
SO CHOOSE YOUR WORDS WISELY
AND MOST IMPORTANTLY
SPEAK FROM YOUR HEART
AND THE WORDS
WILL COME

. . .

CHAPTER 8

What If I Barely Know Them?

W HILE PLAYING THIS GAME, you might have people amongst you that you or others don't really know. That is ok. You can play this game with anyone. Even if you just recently met a person and spent only a few minutes with them, you can do it. When you drop into your heart, you can always find kindness there. You can always see things you appreciate or love about someone, even if you don't know their depth. There is always something that is wonderful, that you can reflect back to another.

Stay in your heart, as your head might jump in trying to find something clever to say. For example, your brother brings his new girlfriend for dinner and you just met her and now you are all going to play this game. You start freaking out. You want to say something nice and smart, but what?

Stop. Get out of your head. Drop into your heart. Think of this beautiful person and reflect all that you appreciate about her. You can always find 5 Things You LOVE About Them if you allow your heart to do the talking. You will become closer to a stranger faster than you could have possibly imagined and both of you will feel super great inside. This game is an incredible way to welcome someone in to your family or friendship circles.

CHAPTER 9

Playing One On One

THE MOST POWERFUL WAY, I think, to play this game is one on one when you are together and in a quiet uninterrupted space. It is perfect to play with your lover, partner, significant other, your parents, your kids, your friends and coworkers.

You tell them 5 Things You LOVE About Them and they tell you 5 Things They LOVE About YOU.

Sometimes, we can live for years with someone but never tell them what we really love about them. Sometimes we sleep every night beside a person but never take the time to tell them or they don't take the time to tell us. Yes we love each other, yet what are the deeper details of why and what? This is where the true intimacy and deep connection occurs, when we can share our hearts so deeply with another and be brave enough to speak love to them and also be brave enough to receive love from them.

This game played one on one can be incredibly healing for your relationships. You might feel really nervous and scared to play with people in your life in this intimate way. But what have you got to lose? More years of a shallow surface relationship that is slowly leaking your life force? Deepen it now. Be brave enough to make this move and deepen your relationship with this game. Allow healing, more love and inspiration to enter your relationships. You know you want it. In the past you might have been too scared to go get it or to receive it, but now you are brave. You are worthy and it is your birthright to be loved.

CHAPTER 10

Playing As A Group

P LAYING AS A GROUP is how I played this game at Christmas. You can put people's names in a hat or take turns focusing your energy on one person. You can continue with the 5 Things I LOVE About YOU or play 1 Thing I LOVE About YOU, if there is a big group of you. When we played at Christmas, we each said 1 thing we loved about the person in receiving. It moved along a lot faster and was an easier start for most people. You can also play 3 Things I LOVE About YOU or 10 or 20. It is up to you.

This game isn't just for Christmas gatherings. It started there because it was when all of my family were together in one place. You can play this game anywhere and everywhere. Play it at the dinner table every night or every week. Play it as you hang out with friends in your living room or sit around a camp fire. Play it on road trips. Play it in your work places and in your classrooms. Play it where ever you gather with others to help inspire each other. It is a powerful and inspiring way to spend your time together.

Kids really love this game, so make sure you include them. Play these kinds of games and start these loving, inspiring and empowering traditions early in children's lives. At an early age, you are teaching your children the art of giving, receiving, verbalizing love, authentic intimacy and gratitude. Your kids will grow up with an appreciation of others and the ability to speak love without fear or embarrassment.

So don't wait until Christmas to play. Play now and play often. Play at every dinner table. Play before you go to bed. Play when you wake up. Play when you text or write a note. Play with your lover. Play with your parent. Play with your child. Play with your friend. Play with your neighbor. Play with anyone you are willing to expand your heart with.

CHAPTER 11

Playing As Focused Energy

THIS IS AN AWESOME WAY to play when you want to focus love and energy on one person. Maybe it is their birthday. Maybe they are celebrating something. Maybe you want to lift them up. Even if no one else knows how to play this game, you can introduce it and invite everyone to play. Maybe you have to start first to lead by example.

I recently got the download to play this game during a yoga studio celebration. We were celebrating a yoga studio's 5th year anniversary but really, we were celebrating the woman who created, birthed and nurtured this studio everyday. With so much focus on the celebration and all the participants having a great time, I decided to introduce this game at the end of the evening so we could focus our energy on the Queen and remind her of her greatness. Beautifully we all shared love and inspiration towards her. It expanded her heart, she felt seen, special and more inspired. All the rest of the participants loved the game too and I invited all of them to play it with their loved ones at their next family dinner.

Some felt an instant yes, yet others hesitated and couldn't visualize this game going down well with their families. As healing as they knew it would be, they feared bringing this powerful magical medicine forth to their families.

So again I invite you, be brave and go for it.

Teachers, please play this game in your classrooms. Most kids have terrible relationships in school with other students, feel insecure in their own skin and uncomfortable in the school system. Allowing each student a moment in the receiving seat and having other children reflect their greatness, could end bullying forever.

Bosses, please play this game in your workplaces. Imagine not only honoring your employee of the month with a plaque or free month of parking, but all of you actually create time to verbally acknowledge the greatness of this individual. Your productivity levels would go up and your turn over rates would go down, as people started to feel more appreciated and acknowledged in their work place.

Yoga teachers, retreat facilitators, group healers, play this game in your big groups or have people break up into smaller groups. This will create much more bond, connection and deepen the transformation process of your students.

Friends play this together. At parties, dinners, baby showers, weddings, engagement parties, birthdays and any time you get together to honor the super important humans you have in your life.

Families do this around the dinner table and honor one person every week. And start sitting down to eat food together if you don't already do so. Create time to be together, to connect to each other and to play the 5 Things I LOVE About YOU game with the most important people in your life.

Remember you actually want love and connection. You want to be seen. You want to be heard. You want to be loved and appreciated. You want to be witnessed for your greatness. Make the time to play this game and become the instigator to play it with everyone. Your willingness can help transform another's life, including your own.

Also don't be shy to ask people to play this game to honor you. If it is your birthday or something special you are celebrating, ask your group of friends to play this game to honor you. Ask them to each tell you one thing they love and adore about you. Don't be shy to ask. It is your birthright to feel loved and special. They might not know about this game, since they don't have this book but you do, so ask for what you want. Don't be shy. You are worth it and they will LOVE giving to you because they LOVE you.

ASK FOR WHAT YOU WANT

DON'T BE SHY

YOU ARE WORTH IT

YOU ARE LOVED

. . .

CHAPTER 12

The Game In Action

HOPEFULLY BY NOW YOU CAN SEE, how easy it is to create an incredible exchange of energy between you and other human beings. All it takes is, your bravery to instigate it. You are brave. It is no accident you have this book in your hand. You have just learned a powerful healing tool that will make your life more magical and much more happy. So you have a choice. You can put this book down and forget we ever met or you can start using this powerful game to help all the relationships in your life. You will be happier and so will all those around you.

Now I'm inviting you in to view my make believe private conversation between my dad and I, as we play the 5 Things I LOVE About YOU game. It may make it easier for you to fully understand how to play, if you can witness the game in action.

Petra speaks first. Dad receives.

Petra: "Sweet Daddy, the first thing I love about you is... how resourceful and handy you are. You can make furniture, camperize a van, create a beautiful garden, race boats, sew clothes and figure most stuff out."

Petra: "Sweet Daddy, the second thing I love about you is... how creative and artistic you are. You make beautiful totem poles with a chain saw. You are very talented."

Petra: "Sweet Daddy, the third thing I love about you is... how determined you are. You accidentally sliced off the tips of your fingers with a table saw and yet with a daily painful practice, you relearned how to play guitar with them."

Petra: "Sweet Daddy, the fourth thing I love about you is... how funny and charismatic you are. At times you are larger than life and can have a whole room silent listening attentively to your jokes and roaring full belly laughs along with you."

Petra: "Sweet Daddy, the fifth thing I love about you is... you are a really good daddy. You have always been present, played guitar to put me to sleep as a child and have always been there to help me. Even when your attentiveness doesn't show up like I may want, I know you always have my back."

Dad speaks next. Petra receives.

Sweet Daddy: "Petrusko, the first thing I love about you is... how wild and free you are with how you live your life and how you love others. Your heart is very big, you believe everyone deserves love and you give it."

Sweet Daddy: "Petrusko, the second thing I love about you is... your bravery to travel, live in different countries and create multiple homes around the world. You are strong and courageous."

Sweet Daddy: "Petrusko, the third thing I love about you is... you are beautiful. You are a beautiful girl. You look amazing for your age and you are very beautiful on the inside too."

Sweet Daddy: "Petrusko, the fourth thing I love about you is... how easy and light you are about life. How easy it is to be around you and how much you uplift me and everyone you come into contact with."

Sweet Daddy: "Petrusko, the fifth thing I love about you is... that I get to say you are mine. I am very proud of the woman you have become and all the beautiful things you do in the world. My friends tell me they think you are amazing and I am proud to say yes I know, she is my daughter."

YOU ARE BRAVE
IT IS NO ACCIDENT
YOU HAVE THIS BOOK
IN YOUR HAND

YOU HAVE LEARNED
A POWERFUL HEALING TOOL
NOW USE IT
GO GET WHAT YOU WANT
DEEP INTIMATE CONNECTION

GO BE SEEN
GO BE HEARD
GO BE LOVED

. . .

CHAPTER 13

Don't Over Complicate This

THE MOST IMPORTANT PART OF PLAYING the 5 Things I LOVE About YOU game, is to make it fun and simple. If you think too much about it, get stressed that you can't do it or you can't say it, then it is not fun. Allow yourself to make this light and fun. Allow yourself to use this game as an experiment into yourself and into the hearts of others all around you. If you allow yourself to witness your emotions, your reactions and your fears, then you can use this game as an opportunity for growth. If you allow yourself to witness other people's reactions and their fears, then you can find more love and compassion for another.

I love being a witness to myself and to life all around me. It makes my life so much more fun to be looking, wondering and questioning. I always look for ways I can up level myself and become a happier, more peaceful human being. I invite you to use this game as an opportunity to find deeper intimacy with yourself and with others. Give yourself permission to dive deep and see what lingers in the depths of your soul.

The example conversation I gave you with my dad was lengthy and filled with many examples. You don't have to go so deep or so long. You can state one thing. You can give a simple example or explanation or not. However you play is up to you. Maybe every time you play, it will be different and maybe every person you play with, will be different too.

The main thing is, just start. Tell someone what you love about them. Even if they don't feel comfortable to give it back to you, who cares? You don't need it. You already love and adore yourself and know how amazing you are. So be the bigger light and give love. Share with others their greatness so they remember it within themselves.

When I played with my dad the first time privately in the car, he said he didn't want to play. So I said, "fine you don't have to play but I will play and I will tell you 5 Things I LOVE About YOU." So I did. He loved it and wanted more and more and more. Sometimes it's up to us, as the bigger light, to give love to others even when they cannot give the verbal affirmation back to us.

It is important however, as the big lights we are, that we do find others who can give back to us. When we only give, eventually it will deplete us. So it is important for us to receive this loving energy and also fill up our soul. It is not healthy to give and give and give, so we have to find those who are brave enough to give back to us. Receiving these affirmative words will replenish your energy battery, as long as you can receive them.

You are an energetic being filled with energy. Sometimes your energy fades, diminishes or depletes. So you have to charge yourself back up. Positive words, experiences and people can help fill you back up. Eating raw vegetables, fruits, green leaves, juices and green smoothies, which are filled with sunshine energy, are the fastest ways you can fuel yourself with light on the inside, along with your own empowering thoughts and self love beliefs.

IT IS UP TO YOU, HOW YOUR LIFE IS. IF YOUR LIFE IS NOT AS GREAT AS YOU WOULD LIKE IT TO BE, THEN DO THESE 3 THINGS TO CHANGE IT...

1. Play this game with people all around you.

2. Read my first book, *"I Am Amazing - A No-Nonsense Self Love Guide To Remember Your Greatness & Rock Out Your Life!"*, to remind yourself of your power and greatness and reprogram your mind for self love and self empowerment. Read with a sponge mind, do the excercises at the end of the chapters and create more peace and happiness within. Buy on Amazon.

3. Join my online programs and in person Bali Retreats, to remind yourself of who you are as a human on this planet and learn how to manifest your ideal life, using your manifesting powers. Remember to be healthy, vibrant and thriving while creating a successful life and business that makes you money while you are sleeping. The super humans that join my coaching are ready to take their life into their hands and be the best version of themselves. Sign up at EatJuicy.com

...

CHAPTER 14

Time To Say
Good Bye

I THINK IT'S TIME TO SAY GOOD BYE and set you free to fly. I've shown you this game. I've empowered you. I've inspired you. I've taught you a few things. You are ready.

The greatest gift I can give you, is remind you of your power as a human creator on this planet. You are not as small as the system would have you believe. You are powerful. You are a miracle of energy living inside a skin bag and you are the most incredible super computer on the planet. You are capable of creating and manifesting anything you desire with the power of your imagination and your willingness to receive. This life is not happening to you but you are creating it. With every thought you think, breath you breathe, word you speak and belief you have. Your life is your creation. This is your movie, your dream, your out picturing reality. You are making it up as you go along. This is your holographic imagined universe that you have created with your mind and you are living inside of it. So let go of victim consciousness and take full control of your life and every relationship in it. This life is your journey so live it fully.

Your journey on this planet is to continue opening to more RECEIVING and LOVING YOURSELF more in the process. If you are putting focus anywhere else, although seemingly important, you are missing the GOLDEN TREASURE. Everything else will fall into place when you focus your energy on LOVING YOURSELF and opening yourself to RECEIVING more bliss. Focus on creating your happy life and magic will happen. Everything you desire is all around you. If you are too afraid to receive it or don't believe you are worthy to receive it, then it won't be magnetized into our reality. So practice receiving with your imagination. Believe it. Dream it. See it as already so.

Learn to love and adore yourself as your bestest friend. This is crucial to living an extraordinary life. Your self love journey will keep going right up until you die. You will always find new ways to love yourself and to fall deeper in love with yourself. So keep growing. Look at all your life situations, all your relationships and ask yourself if you are truly being loving to yourself in all moments. If you are not, then make some changes. Your life is a journey, keep making changes, keep growing, keep expanding, keep receiving and keep loving yourself more until you die.

Self love and opening to receiving more goodness that is all around you, is your soul purpose on this planet. Nothing else.

Everything else is fluff on top of this. It is all an inside job. It is up to you, how amazing or how not so amazing your life is. You can look to other people to change but truly it is up to you. You cannot change another, yet you can change you and then inspire them to join you.

Is this world a scary place or a loving place? The answer is up to you based on the glasses you look through in every moment. If you look for fear, you will find it. If you look for love, you will find it too. The world has both. They are usually happening simultaneously. If you focus all your energy on the not so good stuff, then this is what you will see and more will come. So change your focus to the good stuff, see it all around you and more of it will come.

Every day drop into your heart and take a moment to find gratitude for your life and for your existence on this planet. Be grateful you have another day that life is breathing you and that you get to exist on beautiful miraculous planet earth. Drop in. Put your hand on your heart and drop into the present moment of where you are right now. Give thanks for this moment, for this life you have, for this incredible body that is housing you and for your reality.

Daily count or journal 10 things you are grateful for. Look for the good and find the good. Always find the good in every situation, in every relationship, in every person and in every sadness. Even when it is not easy, look for the good. It will always be there along with the icky stuff.

Find compassion for others. Stop judgment. Find forgiveness and love. Everyone is doing their best on this planet. Even if they are causing harm, they are still doing the best they can in the state they are in. Find love and peace towards others. Be a compassionate, loving, easy going person. Forgive. Let crap go. Don't hang on to the pain for too long, as it will cause YOU harm. Find deep love and compassion for yourself first and then it will come easier for others. Step into your power and shine your light.

Remember you are star light inside a skin bag. You may have chosen to dim your light in the past or others have bullied you to dim it. So set yourself free and remember you are light. Shine! Shine! Shine! No longer shall you fear the dimming from others or the darkness they hold. Shine your light so bright that you give others permission to shine brighter too.

Play the 5 Things I LOVE About YOU game. It will help you shine and help all those around you shine brighter too.

I am happy to be on this journey with you. Thank you for taking the time to read and connect with yourself. May your energy be lighter, brighter, freer and more full of love. May you remember your power and sovereignty as a human on this planet and never allow anyone to dim your light, ever again.

Deep gratitude to you my friend.

Much love and aloha,
Petra

CHAPTER 15

Extraordinary Life Resources

MAY THESE BOOKS AND PROGRAMS INSPIRE YOU to live a more extraordinary, happy, blissed out, abundant, healthy, self healing, miraculous and sovereign life.

I Am Amazing; A No Nonsense Self Love Guide To Remember Your Greatness And Rock Out Your Life

My first book. This book is you reading to yourself from the I AM perspective and reprogramming your own mind and belief system in the process. I AM are the two most powerful words in your vocabulary and the words you put after them are even more powerful. I am amazing or I am stupid. You get to choose your reality. This book is a powerful tool for you to live your most healthy, happy and empowered life as a human on this planet. Found on Amazon and Kindle.

Detox Me Juicy; A 7 Day Juicy Food Cleanse To Lose Weight, Youthen & Heal Your Body Of Everything
This book is a step by step guide for you to do a juice and juicy food cleanse from the comfort of your home. You will learn how to cleanse and detox your body, give your digestion a break and restart your system. Your body is always trying to heal you, it is time for you to get on board and help your body get there faster. You can heal from all sickness, lose weight and look years younger by following my guidance. Also written in the I Am perspective so you can reprogram your brain and integrate all the ideas suggested. Found on Amazon and Kindle

Green Smoothie Gangster Lifestyle Program
Get super food recipes and action steps to transition to a juicier lifestyle this simple doable way. Make SUPER FOOD smoothies for breakfast, slowly lose weight and keep it off. No chemical powder shakes or speed pills. These are recipes that will clean you out, heal your gut, get rid of constipation and lose your fat forever. You will feel good in your clothes, feel lighter in your body and have energy to live your life. Over the next 40 days you will gain more confidence, a peaceful mind, radical self love and personal empowerment. It's time to take your health into your hands and this weight loss program will get you there... I guarantee it! Sign up at GreenSmoothieGangster.com

Petra's Juicy Lifestyle, Business & Health Club For Women
Join QUEEN BEE SCHOOL. Live more fully in your womanly power, connect deeper to your intuition, feel amazing in your body and make money while you are sleeping doing what lights you up. Remind yourself of who you are as a woman on this planet and how to wield your feminin manifesting powers. Remember to be healthy, vibrant and thriving while creating a successful life and business you love. The super women that join this coaching are ready to take their life into their hands and be the best version of themselves. Sign up at EatJuicy.com

Cancer Is Not A Monster Coaching Program
As you know healing from cancer and preventing cancer is near and dear to my heart since my mom died from cancer and I self healed myself of it. So I created videos, audios, recipes, lessons and resources to support you on your cancer healing journey so you don't feel alone and you have someone who has your back. A lack of information and feeling lost, confused and alone is the scariest place you can be. I don't want any of you to feel panicked and frantically searching everywhere for information or the possible cure. When we tried healing my mom naturally, we knew nothing and grasped everywhere looking for her healing. It is my intention and desire for you to find some safety, security and deep inner knowing in this program, so you know how to heal your cancer naturally and you are safe. You can heal yourself. Your body is a self healing machine and is working for your healing 24/7. You just need to know what to do to give it a little help. This program will help you do that. Learn as much as you can and give yourself the faith that you can heal from your cancer. Sign up at EatJuicy.com

Stay tuned for more books and programs that I am creating for you. Next will be the Eat Juicy Cook Book, then the Green Smoothie Gangster Recipe and tour book will soon be available.

You can find more support, recipes, inspirations and helpful juicy lifestyle tips on Petra EatJuicy social media.

Much love and light to you. I love you. Thank you for allowing me into your reality and being willing to be the BIGGEST SELF EXPRESSION of YOURSELF on this planet and to have the greatest life.

YOU ARE AMAZING
YOU ARE POWERFUL
YOU ARE INFINITE
YOU ARE ENOUGH

. . .

Petra EatJuicy is a Super Hero Level Holistic Health Coach, Detox Expert, Author, Raw Food Chef, Theta Healing Practitioner and Intuitive Flow Yoga Teacher. She travels the world speaking, teaching and coaching about natural eating, self healing, mindfulness, radical self love and personal empowerment. She and her team tour the world empowering people to take their health into their own hands...She lives in Bali, Maui, Canada and Czech Republic.

Check out her amazing online coaching programs to reverse cancer, heal your gut, lose weight without counting calories, make money while sleeping and live your most vibrant self expressed life.

www.EatJuicy.com
www.GreenSmoothieGangster.com

www.Facebook.com/PetraEatJuicy
www.Youtube.com/PetraEatJuicy
www.Instagram.com/PetraEatJuicy

I Am Amazing

A No-Nonsense Self Love Guide To Remember Your Greatness & Rock Out Your Life! Empower Yourself, Feel Happier, Heal Your Body & Become Your Own Best Friend

- Petra EatJuicy, Green Smoothie Gangster

5 Things I Love About You

A Game For You To Heal Your Relationships With Everyone

- Petra EatJuicy, Green Smoothie Gangster

Detox Me Juicy

A 7 Day Juicy Food Cleanse To Lose Weight, Youthen & Heal Your Body Of Everything

- Petra EatJuicy, Green Smoothie Gangster

We are a Gang
Healing the Planet

Join Us!

eatjuicy.com

♥love your life♥

Green Smoothie Gangster.com

Made in United States
North Haven, CT
25 August 2023

40763053R00050